Illuminating Light: Reignite Your Essence

J. Lenitiva

Illuminating Light: Reignite Your Essence
© 2023 J. Lenitiva

All rights reserved.

No part of this publication may be reproduced, stored in a retrieval system, or transmitted, in any form or by any means, electronic, mechanical, photocopying, recording, or otherwise, without the prior written permission of the presenters.

J. Lenitiva asserts the moral right to be identified as the author of this work.

Presentation by *BookLeaf Publishing*

Web: www.bookleafpub.com

E-mail: info@bookleafpub.com

ISBN: 9789357440288

First edition 2023

DEDICATION

You did it babe. The days you wanted to quit, you finally made it. One of your hardest years, yet, you pushed. Alotta shit came at you, I know you wanted to break. There were times you thought to leave this world, but we are in too deep. It's gonna be okay. You're going to smile again. You're going to find your happiness. The darkness is going to continue to come, but continue to find the light. Make the best of what you have. Trouble doesn't last always. I know, easier said than done, but believe for as long as you can. The devil will try to make you feel like it's over, but someone bigger, right above, writes your story. You're destined for greatness, just gotta believe. It's okay to not have everything set in stone. Just continue to dream, and act on it. I hope you always keep a smile on your face. That you learn it's okay to make mistakes. That builds character. Be prepared for the worst. Those down moments will come. Shake back. Focus on your happiness. It's your life, your decisions. Love God, your family, your friends, yourself, your plan. Don't forget where you come from. Raised right, shine bright. Never forget what makes you cry, it makes you stronger.

I love you forever, your #1 fan,

Liv and S.S.

ACKNOWLEDGEMENT

To Whom It May Concern,

For anyone that fell in the dark and wants to find the light.
To him, who was my light and happiness in my darkness.
To Squish, Martini, and my Day Ones for pushing me towards my dream
To the Queens, the only family I shared with.... I hope to meet you guys at the top..
J, thank you for being born.
Sunset, you too.
To my home, thank you for the memories you've given me.
I hope I make you proud,
That your only wish is to see me happy.
I'm in the light now, and my darkness is gone

For the most part.. ♥

PREFACE

I'm surprised you were able to find this book.
It's not like myself to show it.
I've always dreamt about this coming true.
I just hope you're not the only one to lay eyes on it.
If I offend you in any way along the way,
I do not apologize.
For that is not my issue or concern.
My goal is to get these thoughts out of my head.
Along the way, my brain might have suffered from overload.
Two options were the walls and the writing.
I chose both…
And both healed over time.

Writing is a good way to comment on life's reality.
May these pieces bring you smiles,
tears,
motivation,
or all of the above.

Acts 17: 28

Thank you,
For being the reason I am here today.
That I am able to experience life more abundantly.
For allowing everything in me to function how you expect it to.
For opening my eyes to see the sunrise and the moonlight.
To feel the love in my heart for the blessings You bring.
Allowing me to speak the words a million times and it STILL NOT BE ENOUGH...
I THANK YOU AND I LOVE YOU!

Beautiful Roller Coaster

It's such a beautiful thing, ya know.
Giving you joy and happiness,
But then when it comes to an end,
You don't want it to.
Most times…
It's better to enjoy the ride,
Instead of cutting it short and ending up
regretting it.
So live and have fun and enjoy this roller
coaster.
Because once it's over,
You get off hoping you can go again.
But the chance won't be there.

To the Girl like Me/GEM

Sometimes...
I feel like I'm not enough.
Mostly because people label me more than enough.
Trying to fit the norm, never really worked.
People can always put their two cents, so I'll apply the 100,
I'm more than enough, never needed your opinion.
The old me would've needed the spare change,
But the new me, you can spare 'cause my mindset is not the same.
I knock down every insensitive reality in society
Because the curves of my shape are just as beautiful, regardless of what you think.
Let my light shine,
May it never go dim.
My body,
EveryBODY is a gem

her.

love.
the rays of the sun,
but also the rain of the storm.
a love that stretches as wide as the sea.
passion.
finding her smile,
never letting it fade.
dream.
to never run out.
regret.
letting anger consume her.
morals.
being true and finding truth.
ambition.
the different dimensions of opportunity.
muse.
simple beauty.
her.

Flick

into the flick of it
up and away
get lost in the flame
so bright I can see Saturn
take me to the moon
into orbit
the fire we make
as the meteors crash down
takes the breath away
as two souls cum as one.

#skyfall

THE SKY IS FALLING! THE SKY IS FALLING!!
That's always my favorite thing to say.
Something so dangerous, yet funny at the same time.
You know that's the same as life.
Deep shit and high waters rise, never knowing what's next.
I have no time to waste, so if I don't feel that the sky is on fire
You aren't the one for me.
I really want you to be.
I think you could be.
But do you want to?
Can you be?
If you don't have faith, how can I?
Two-way streets are better than one. So let's see where they lead.

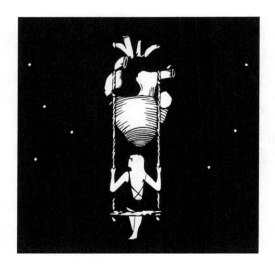

Fairy Tales

In a land of royalty,
Living far, far away,
Is it possible to live in a place of peace?
I'm not saying it's going to be all fairy tales, but let's have the best story we could write.
Our love is a fire that burns forever
A forbidden fruit in the picnic basket of standards
A love that was taken from us
Love that is "not allowed"
Because it's a love that is so strong.
I see the growth in you, you know.
Our love grows so wild because it's so many things against it.
If you like, we could dance to the music all night.
We can argue over sports, or books,
Or who washed dishes last or who's in charge of dinner.
Let's be spontaneous, creative.
Watch movies,
Make movies...
Make something out of nothing that nobody could ever take from us.

Rock n Roll

Make music with me
Be the guitarist and I'm your lead vocalist.
Never lose the beat
Make me into a musical masterpiece.

Good Lovin

It's crazy
I've always wanted a certain kinda love, but never seem to find it.
It's like I want that Martin and Gina type of love, but I always feel like Cole.
Or that Curtis and Ella love, but I'm annoying like Floyd.
That Justice and Lucky love, tho....
NOW that's the best kinda love.
That love you never imagined yourself into.
Sometimes I feel like that kinda love you see in scripts, you'll never see.
Simply because that's what it's meant for...scripts.
But somehow I still have that little bit I hang on to,
Cause maybe someday, I might get that special kinda lovin'
That best friend kinda lovin' like Tupac and Jada
That competitive love like Wade and Gabi
That intimate love like Iman and Teyana
But most of all,
I want that powerful love
Like my Barack and Michelle
Yea, it may be a long shot
But ima still shoot for that genuine, good lovin'.

12:45

The thoughts that run through my mind
Some sensual.
Some sexual...
Most are intellectual babe,
I wanna see what you really think about
If you can trigger my interest for you.
it could all be so simple, me and you,
No phones, no interruptions...
Just the music to let the vibes flow.
The vibes to flow from your lips and mine
I wanna learn more about you
Things from what your childhood was like to what your sex life is like...
I'm sorry...my mind likes to wonder,
But I hope your hands...
I mean your mind will wonder with me.
I feel like I can talk to you forever and never run out of steam.
There are so many mysteries to you and I wanna unlock every one:
Come explore with me and let's see what we can find.

Drunken Fruit

One sip
Two sips...
Two cups, four
The taste of the liquor fades away
How does something so strong not leave a mark?
Is it the juice?
Is it the fruit I add to soak up the strength of the liquors surrounding
Ima pineapple girl..I like the sweetness
Four cups turn into me on the couch with my sixth cup in one hand
My phone in the other...
Typing the things I want to say to you...
The things I wanna do to you..
Hoping your levels match mine.
The liquor loosens me up so the typing is easier and the descriptions get better
They flow from my mind to my fingertips.
Just like I want my juices to flow on your...never mind that.
My cup is empty
Fruit still sits at the bottom
One piece
Two piece
My finger presses send...
Three piece, ten piece
Phone lights up...
Guess it's time for me to come to you…

Rainy Dayz

I sit on my steps and I watch the pure beauty
Nature at its finest
I like to think of it as the cries He's gathered,
releasing them into the Earth
To fall into Earth's soul
And create something beautiful.

Ambient Air

Today I thought about death.
Before judging,
It's not a suicidal thought
But sometimes, I wouldn't mind if that day came...
life can be hard sometimes
and reminding yourself that there's still beauty in it..
Sometimes that doesn't work.
But then I think about the people I wouldn't see again.
Miss their smiles,
Their laughs,
Their love.
But I also miss that with the ones that left too soon.
If only we had wings..

Letter to a Friend

Hi there,
I miss you a lot,
but I know you don't miss me.
You might even wish we never met.
I know I hurt you bad, I just thought you were the one....
I thought we needed each other
Everything moved too quick
And I almost had you,
But you were better than that
I'm glad you were stronger than I thought you were...
Because I know you wouldn't have survived dancing
with a devil like me.

Mental Disruption

Pills and potions
Fulfill your purpose.
Fill me with air so I may float.
High into the sky
I'm so high in my mind
A dream I don't wanna wake up from
I'm happy here
In my magical land
Pills and potions
Call it witchcraft
I mix you together to cast a spell
I never thought it would come to this
My daily demons chasing me
Knowing I can't shake 'em
My body numb
I got sleep paralysis
I paint a smile on my face so my screams won't be heard
I close my eyes and I can't wake up
Drugs got me shaking
Demons get closer and my body freezes
I'll see how long I can dance before I wake…

Time Flies

The fastest thing in the world
I wish it would slow down
Matter of fact, I wish it could rewind
I wanna time travel
Wish superpowers were real
Living with you through pictures
If only they could come alive
That little girl with that big smile in your eyes
The picture doesn't smear, will never fade
Not even after the tears roll onto em
Quick, the clock keeps tickin,
I make my wish
Hoping one day, it'll come true and I'll see you again..

Curtain Call

It happened so fast but I knew this day would come..
I hate this is the last time they'll see me,
But my time had just run its course..
Protect them, for I am no longer with them physically.
Give them strength that only You can give.
During this final goodbye,
Remind them, I'm forever with them..

Puzzle Picture

How can you see yourself if you don't accept all of the pieces?
Do you know what to look for if you never even look at them?
Every detail, every color,
every failure, every success,
From the breakdowns to breakthroughs.
Every piece is critical,
Because it all comes as part of the full package.
The frame isn't meant to hold something of no value.
The pieces might not be perfect,
But remember, everything comes together how it's meant to be.

Either Way

if it gets dark, find light.
if the pieces are crumbling, rebuild
if it feels too much, let go.
if the music is good, dance.
if it feels like butterflies, fly.
If it brings happiness, smile
(now read it again, backwards)

My Letter to U

Say you'll never leave me...
I don't know what I'll do without you.
I felt like for a long time you weren't a part of me...
Thought I lost you for good.
It's like every time I got close to you
Something pulled me away.
I would think we just weren't meant to be.
But I'm glad, sooner or later,
I found a piece of you again.
My spirits are lifting and hopefully, one day,
You'll push the darkness out of my soul.
To you, happiness, I thank you for sticking around.

Self Discovery

Roads of the unknown
That leads to who knows where?
Knowing that there really are stars
that hide behind the clouds..
To love the sound of a new song
Nothing lasts forever, unfortunately
Then again, was it supposed to?
Jump out in fear, it's okay to not know.
Time to discover what the fucks,
Instead of wondering what-ifs.

Printed in the USA
CPSIA information can be obtained
at www.ICGtesting.com
LVHW011118130324
774329LV00015B/886